Everything a Kid Needs to Know about Money

Children's Money & Saving Reference

BABY PROFESSOR

EDUCATION KIDS

Speedy Publishing LLC
40 E. Main St. #1156
Newark, DE 19711
www.speedypublishing.com

Instructions:

Read the amount on each page. Then, cut and paste the coins from the back pages to make each amount on the page.

15 ¢

30 ¢

45 ¢

60 ¢

O O O o or

O o

75 ¢

16 ¢

22 ¢

28 ¢

34 ¢

40 ¢

46 ¢

52 ¢

58 ¢

64 ¢

70 ¢

76 ¢

82 ¢

88 ¢

94 ¢

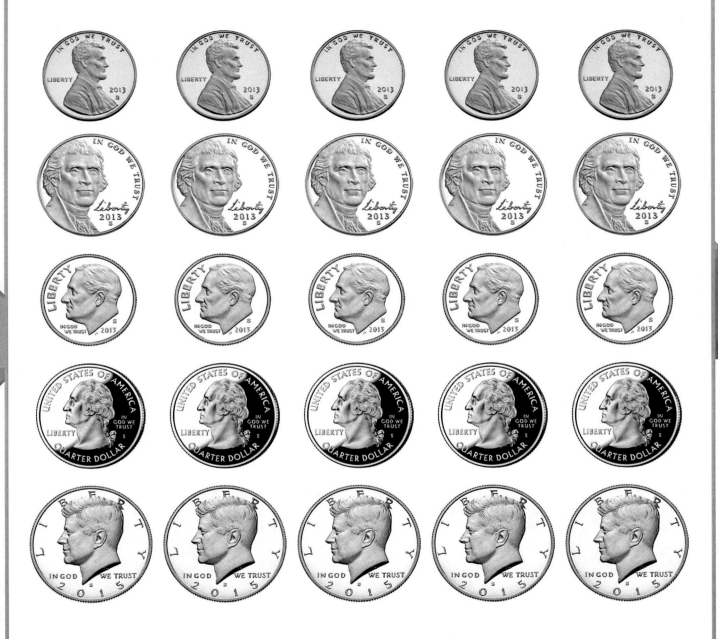

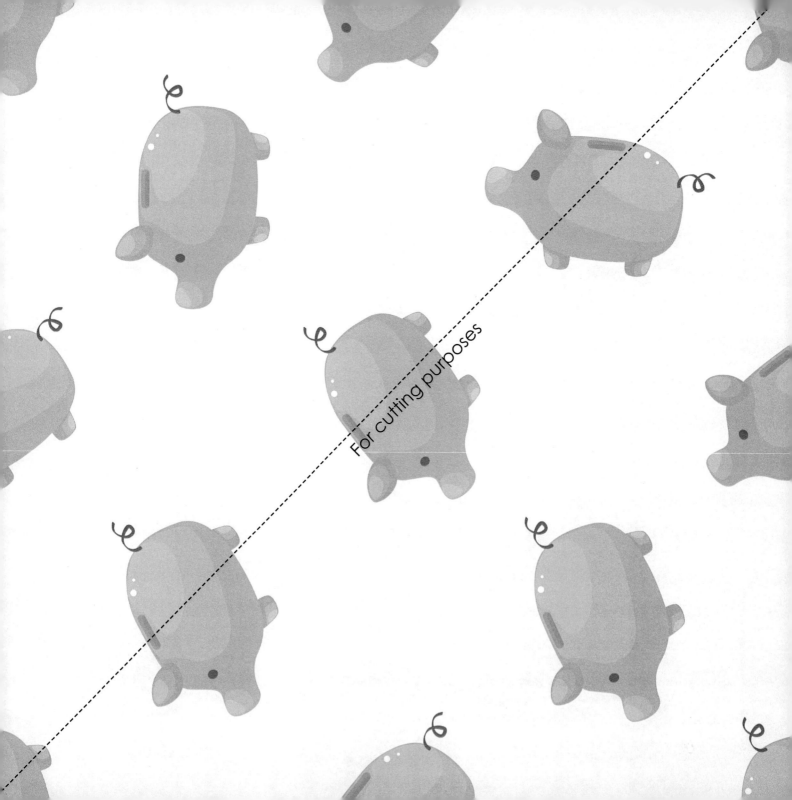

For cutting purposes

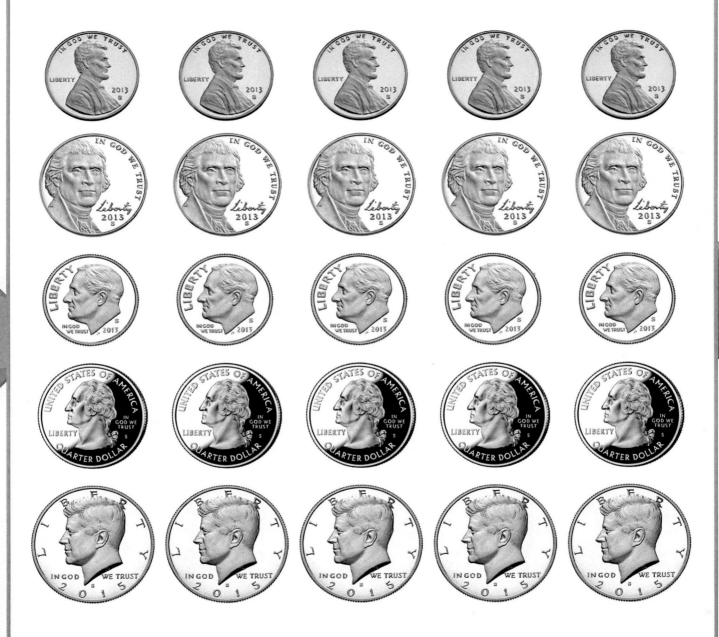

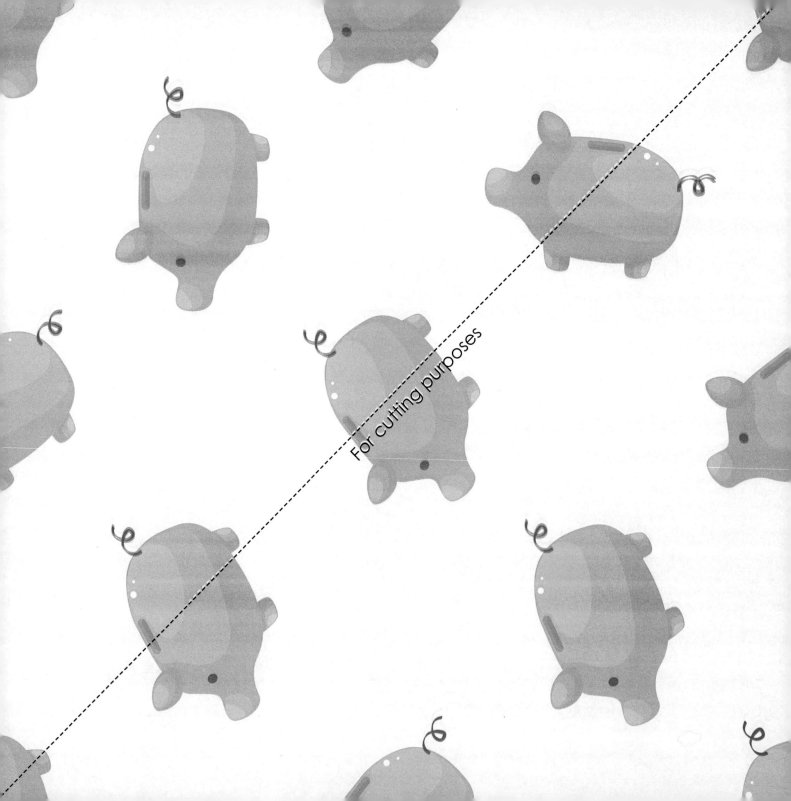

For cutting purposes

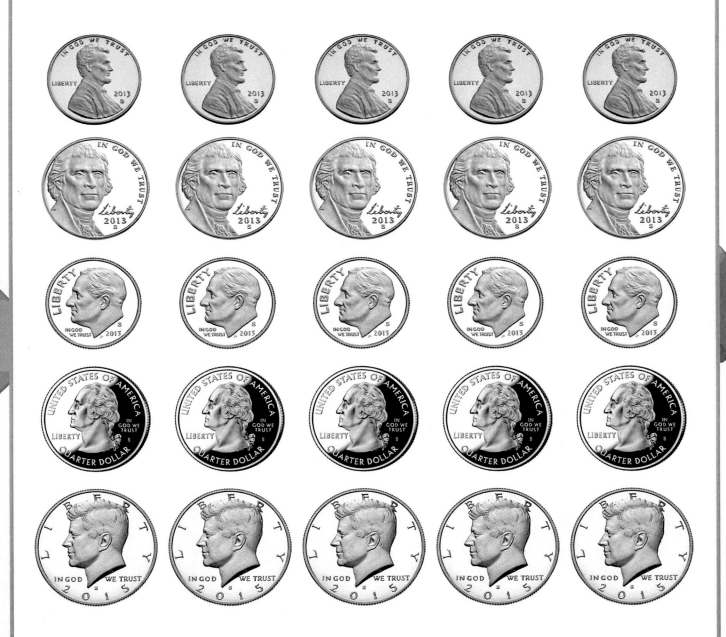

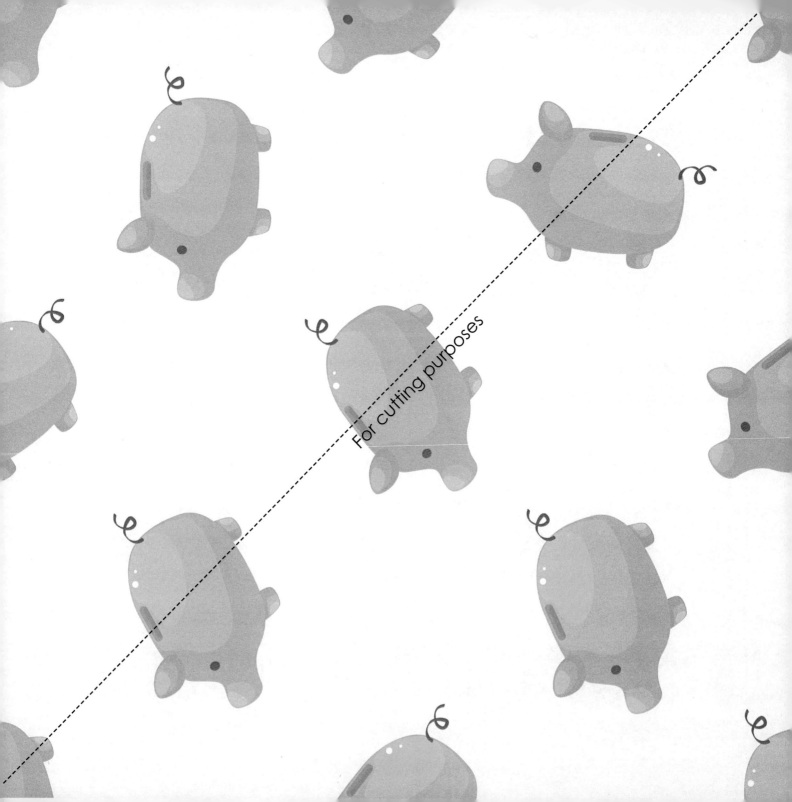

For cutting purposes

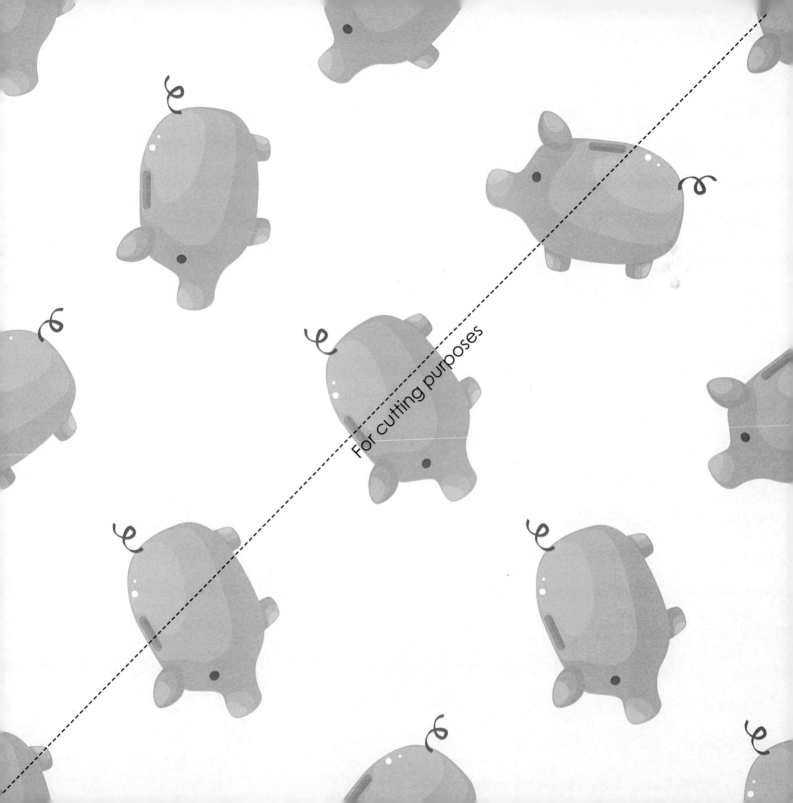

For cutting purposes

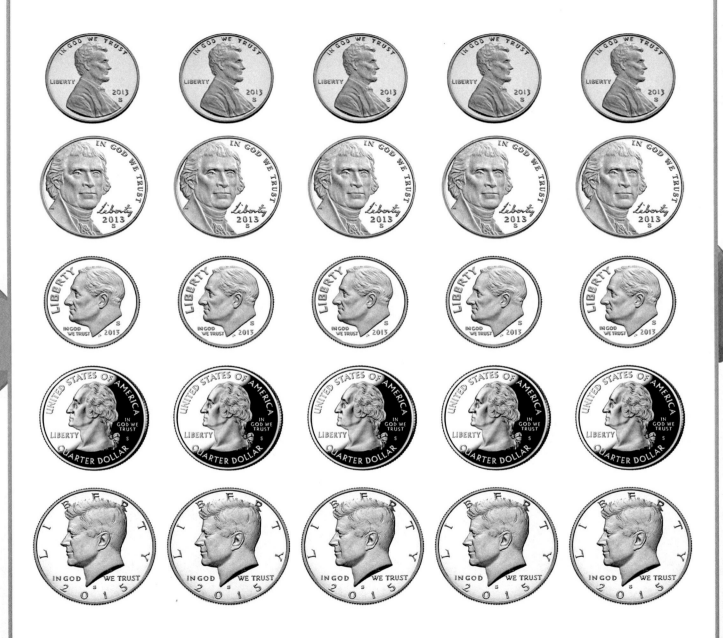

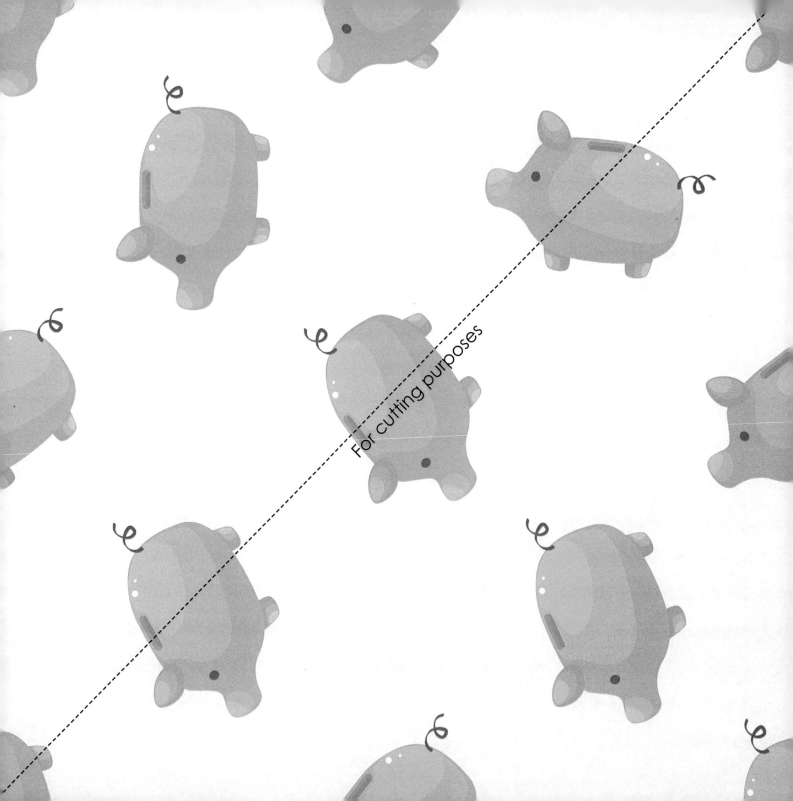

For cutting purposes

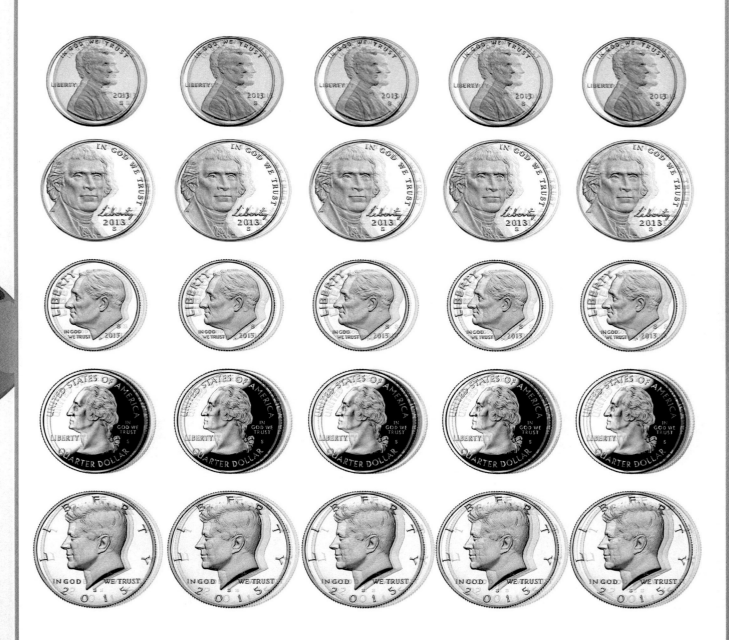

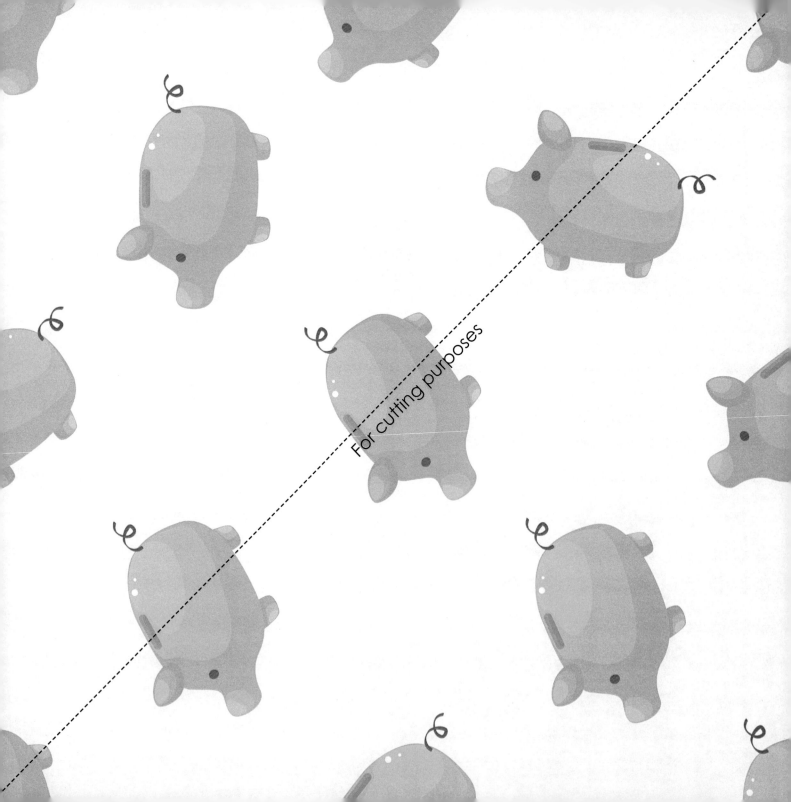

For cutting purposes

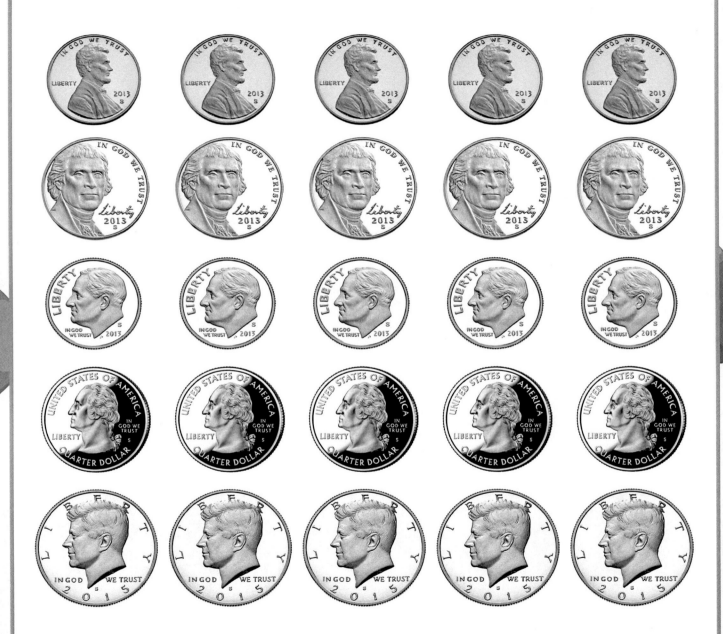

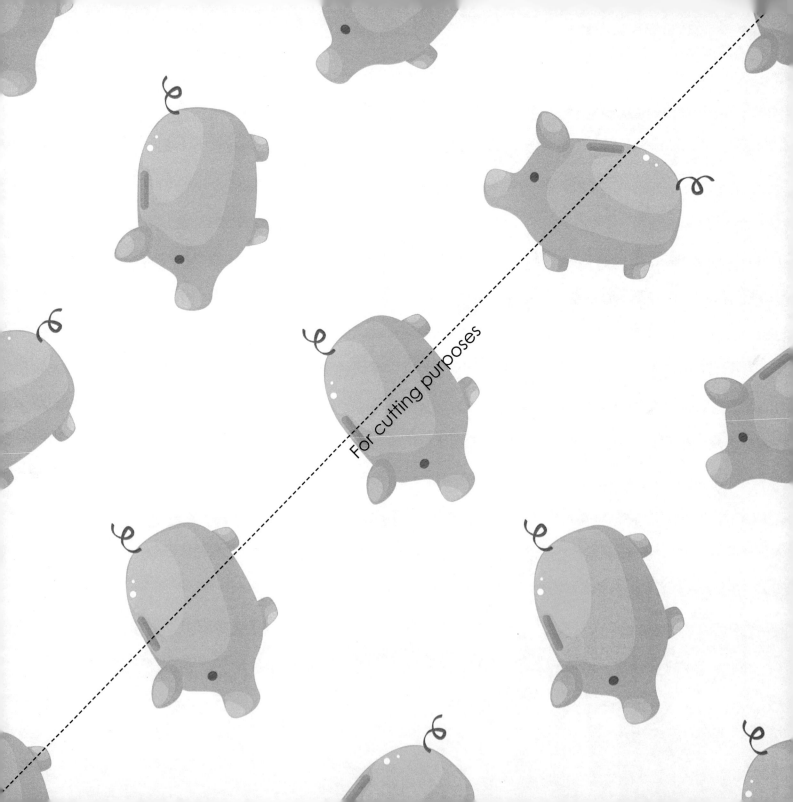

For cutting purposes

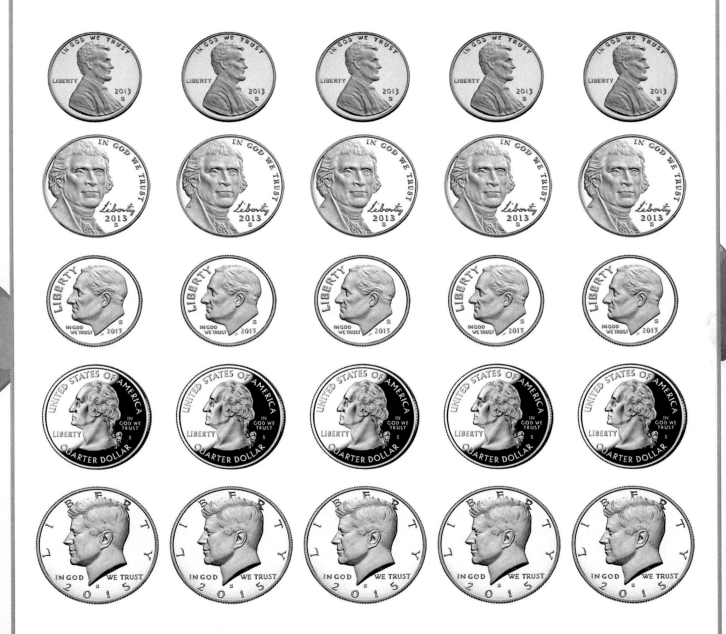

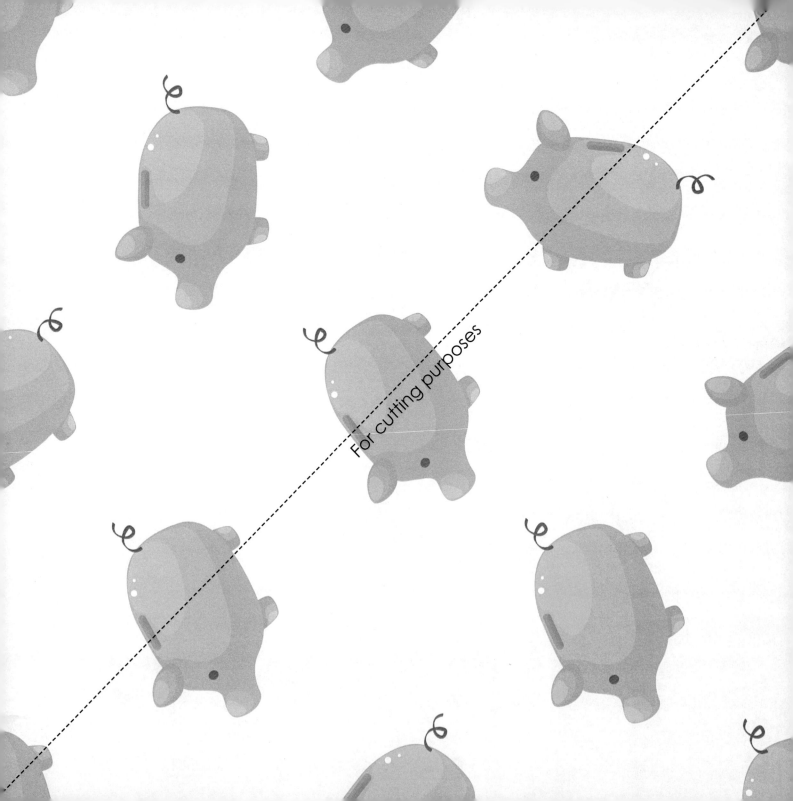

For cutting purposes

Answers may vary.
You may ask your
guardian after
answering if your
answers are correct.

50430968R00025

Made in the USA
San Bernardino, CA
22 June 2017